Thank You,
HELPERS

For Captain Tom, a true hero
—P.H.

For Noah and Matilda
—M.E.

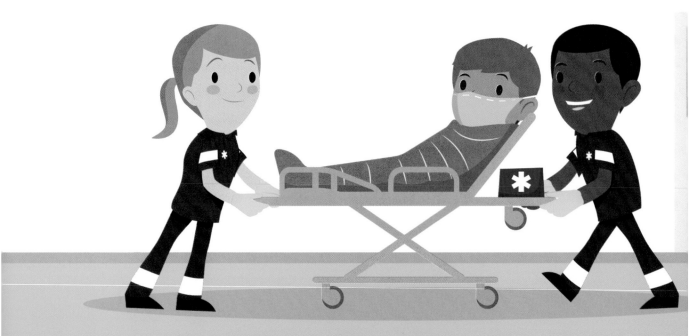

Text copyright © 2020 by Caterpillar Books Ltd
Cover art and interior illustrations copyright © 2020 by Michael Emmerson

All rights reserved. Published in the United States by Random House Children's Books, a division of Penguin Random House LLC, New York.
Published in the United Kingdom by Caterpillar Books, an imprint of the Little Tiger Group, London, in 2020.

Random House and the colophon are registered trademarks of Penguin Random House LLC.

Visit us on the Web!
rhcbooks.com

Educators and librarians, for a variety of teaching tools, visit us at RHTeachersLibrarians.com

Library of Congress Control Number: 2020937429
ISBN 978-0-593-37338-5 (pbk) — ISBN 978-0-593-37339-2 (ebook)

Printed in the United States of America
1 2 3 4 5 6 7 8 9 10
First American Edition

Thank You, HELPERS

By Patricia Hegarty

Illustrated by Michael Emmerson

Random House 🏠 New York

The world is full of

HEROES.

And when
the going gets
tough,

those heroes
all get going.

We can't
thank them enough!

Three cheers for the **DOCTORS** keeping viruses at bay.

You are **heroes**, yes, you are.

Hip-hip-hip-hooray!

Let's hear it FOR THE NURSES, tending patients all day long.

You are **heroes,**
yes, you are.

You're
kind
and **brave**
and
strong!

Here's to PARAMEDICS,
who save so many Lives.

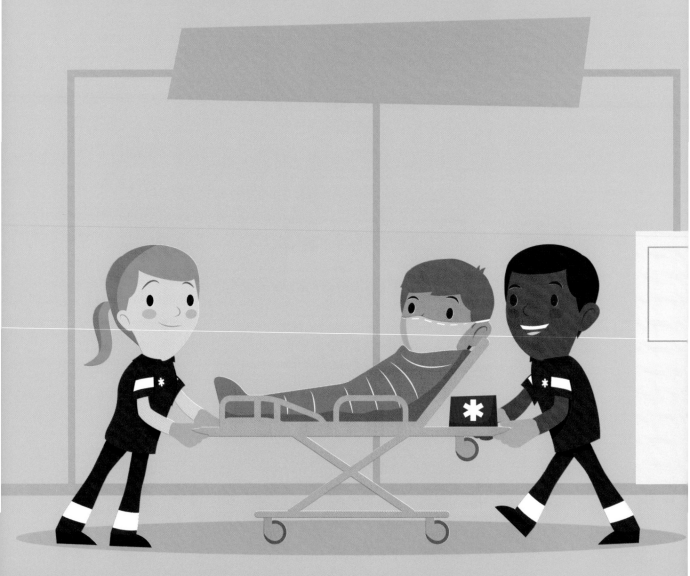

You are **heroes,**
yes, you are.

We're sending you
high fives!

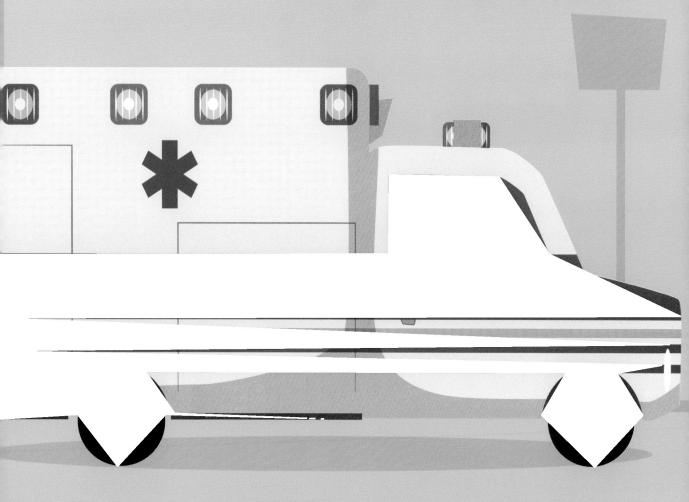

To each
HOSPITAL WORKER,

for
everything you do,

you are
heroes,

yes,
you are.

We **owe** our
thanks to you!

To
CAREGIVERS
for our loved ones,

as you all
play your parts,

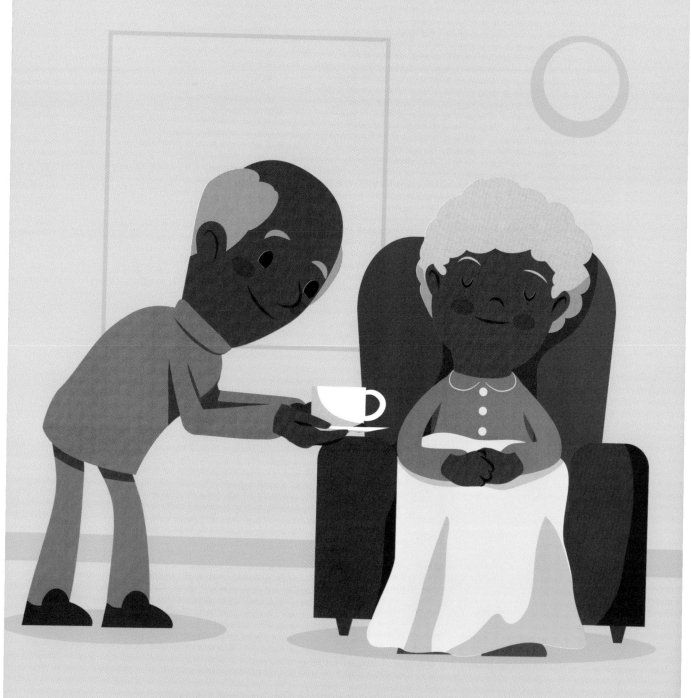

you are **heroes**, yes, you are.
We keep you in **our hearts!**

You are heroes,
yes, you are,

and you
deserve
a
hand!

Thumbs up to all the **WORKERS** in vehicles and in shops.

You are **heroes,**
yes, you are.

PHARMACY

You've pulled out
all the stops!

Hooray for GROCERY WORKERS

in each and every store.

You are **heroes,**
yes, you are.

We couldn't
Love you more!

Let's **not forget** the **TEACHERS**, in **classrooms** and **online**.

You are **heroes,** yes, you are.

You encourage **kids to shine!**

You are **heroes,**
yes, you are.

On that
we all
agree!

We're so **PROUD** of all our

HEROES,

so we **CLaP** and **ShOut** and **Cheer.**

We're all in this **together,**

and we'll **get through it, never fear!**

Meet Some HEROES

Doctors figure out what is wrong with us when we are sick and give prescriptions to help us get better.

Nurses work hard to care for us and make sure we get the medicine and help we need.

Paramedics are on the front line, responding to emergencies, driving ambulances, and saving lives.

Warehouse workers handle the safe packing and delivery of millions of goods from all around the world to our shops and homes.

All the **staff in hospitals** have an important role to play, from the kitchen staff to the porters and the cleaners.

There are millions of **caregivers** looking after loved ones in their own homes or working in nursing homes.

Delivery workers travel far to make sure we all have the things we need.

Volunteers help in the community by delivering food, helping neighbors, and fundraising.

Grocery workers keep the shelves stocked in stores with food and everyday supplies.

Teachers carry on with their lessons in classrooms or online so we can all keep learning.

Our **transportation workers** drive buses and trains so we can get where we need to be.